Hippo
River Horse

by Natalie Lunis

Consultants:

Tony Barthel
Curator, Smithsonian's National Zoological Park

Rebecca Lewison, Ph.D.
Chair, IUCN Hippo Specialist Group;
Assistant Professor, San Diego State University

BEARPORT
PUBLISHING

NEW YORK, NEW YORK

Credits

Cover, © Eric Isselée and ecoventurestravel/Shutterstock; TOC, © Eric Isselée/Shutterstock; 4, © Richard Du Toit/Minden Pictures/SuperStock; 5, © Thomas Dressler/Ardea; 6, © Winfried Wisniewski/The Image Bank/Getty Images; 7, © Mathieu Laboureur/Biosphoto/Peter Arnold/Photolibrary; 9, © Robert Harding Picture Library/SuperStock; 10T, © Ferrero-Labat/Ardea; 10B, © Smithsonian's National Zoo/Mehgan Murphy; 11, © Mark Boulton/Alamy; 12T, © Winfried Wisniewski/FLPA/Minden Pictures; 12B, © Gianni Dagli Orti/Corbis; 13, © Pacific Stock/SuperStock; 14T, © Andrew Parkinson/FLPA/Minden Pictures; 14B, © age fotostock/SuperStock; 15, © ZSSD/Minden Pictures/SuperStock; 16T, © Philip Dalton/Nature Picture Library; 16C, © belizar/shutterstock; 16B, © Vaclav Silha/Barcroft/Fame Pictures; 17, © Tony Heald/Nature Picture Library; 18, © John Warden/Riser/Getty Images; 19, © ZSSD/Minden Pictures/SuperStock; 20–21, © Tim Fitzharris/Minden Pictures/SuperStock; 22, Royalty Free Composite; 23TL, © Tier und Naturfotografie/SuperStock; 23TR, © Moremi/Shutterstock; 23BL, © Anup Shah/age fotostock/SuperStock; 23BR, © Mathieu Laboureur/Biosphoto/Peter Arnold/Photolibrary; 24, © Eric Isselée/Shutterstock.

Publisher: Kenn Goin
Editorial Director: Adam Siegel
Creative Director: Spencer Brinker
Cover Design: Dawn Beard Creative and Kim Jones
Photo Researcher: Picture Perfect Professionals, LLC

Library of Congress Cataloging-in-Publication Data

Lunis, Natalie.
  Hippo : river horse / by Natalie Lunis.
     p. cm. — (Animal loudmouths)
  Includes bibliographical references and index.
  ISBN-13: 978-1-61772-275-2 (library binding)
  ISBN-10: 1-61772-275-8 (library binding)
  1. Hippopotamus—Juvenile literature. I. Title.
  QL737.U57L86 2012
  599.63'5—dc22
                              2011002426

For more information, write to Bearport Publishing Company, Inc., 45 West 21st Street, Suite 3B, New York, New York 10010. Printed in the United States of America in North Mankato, Minnesota.

070111
042711CGB

10 9 8 7 6 5 4 3 2 1

Contents

A Loud Roar

In the shallow part of a river, two hippopotamuses stand face-to-face.

Each one holds its huge mouth open.

Suddenly, one hippo swings its head, scoops up some water, and hurls it at the other.

Then it lets out a roar.

The sound is as loud as a train engine.

A hippo's mouth is huge. When open, it measures about four feet (1.2 m) from top to bottom. That's big enough for a six-year-old child to stand up inside.

Fighting and Biting

Why is the hippo in the river roaring?

He is fighting with another male to defend his **territory**.

During a fight, each animal roars, snorts, grunts, and honks to scare the other.

Usually, one of the hippos backs off and leaves.

Sometimes, however, the angry hippos use their huge front teeth to attack each other.

A fight between two male hippos can last for hours.

Herds of Hippos

Hippos are some of the loudest and noisiest animals in Africa.

They don't make noise only when they fight, however.

Hippos live in groups called herds.

The members of a herd call to one another by snorting and **bellowing**.

With its call, each animal says, "Here I am!"

Sometimes all the hippos in a herd join together to make the same sound.

Hippos in the Wild

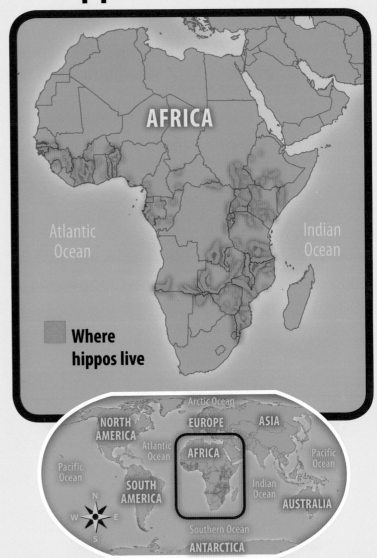

AFRICA

Atlantic Ocean

Indian Ocean

Where hippos live

Arctic Ocean

NORTH AMERICA

EUROPE

ASIA

Atlantic Ocean

AFRICA

Pacific Ocean

Pacific Ocean

SOUTH AMERICA

Indian Ocean

AUSTRALIA

Southern Ocean

ANTARCTICA

hippo herd

Staying Cool

Hippos live in grassy areas of Africa where there are lakes or rivers.

During the day, the big animals stay in the water—and out of the hot sun.

They need to do so to keep their rough, gray skin from drying out and cracking.

pink sweat

Unlike people, hippopotamuses cannot make watery sweat to cool off their bodies. They do, however, give off an oily pink liquid through their skin. It helps protect a hippo's skin from drying out and from sunburn.

River Horses

Hippopotamuses got their name because they spend so much of their time in the water.

The word *hippopotamus* comes from two ancient Greek words meaning "river" and "horse."

Today, scientists do not think of hippos as close relatives of horses.

Instead, they have found that hippos are more closely related to whales.

ancient Egyptian hippo statue

Thousands of years ago, hippos lived in the Nile River in Egypt. The ancient Egyptians hunted the animals. They also made many pieces of artwork that showed how the animals looked.

humpback
whale

Eating All Night

At night, hippos leave the water to find food.

They head for nearby places where grasses grow.

They use their big, strong lips to tear the grass and push it into their mouths.

They use big, flat teeth at the back of their mouths to chew up the grass.

When the sun comes up, they go back to the water to rest and stay cool.

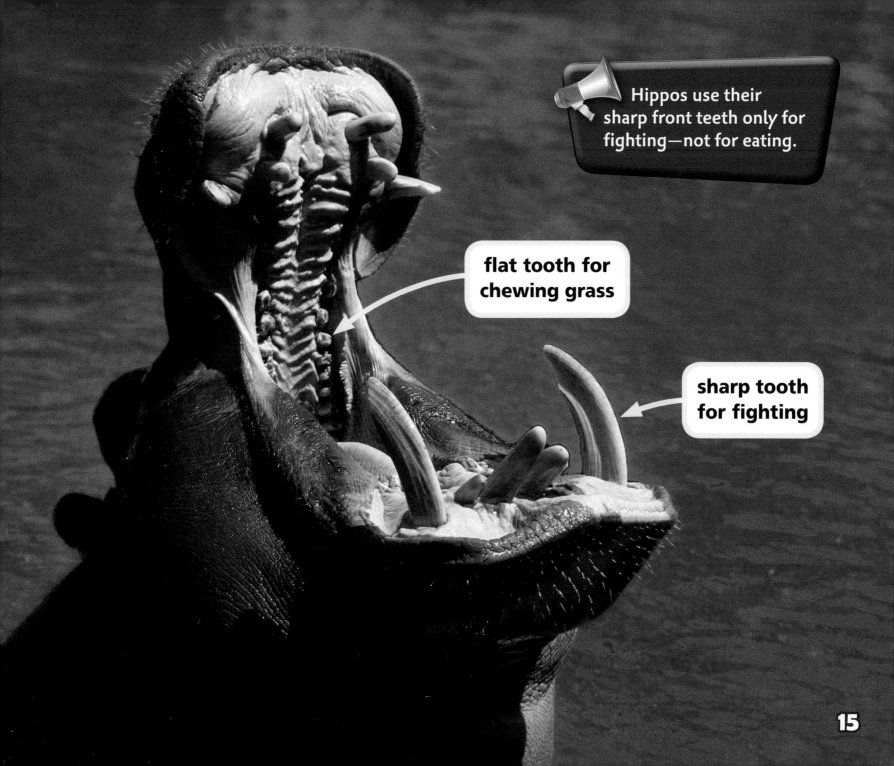

Dealing with Danger

Because adult hippos are so big, they do not have any real enemies—either in the water or on land.

Baby hippos, however, are sometimes hunted by lions, hyenas, and crocodiles.

Luckily, mother hippos are always watching for danger.

If they spot it, they take quick action.

A mother hippo can run straight toward a lion or hyena and chase it away.

She can bite a crocodile in half.

lion

hyena

crocodile

Baby hippos weigh up to 100 pounds (45 kg) when they are born. Adult males can weigh up to 5,800 pounds (2,631 kg). Adult females are smaller than males. They weigh about 3,000 pounds (1,361 kg).

mother hippo

baby hippo

Sound All Around

Since ancient times, people have known that hippos are big, fierce, and loud.

However, in the past few years, scientists have learned some surprising things about them.

One discovery is that hippos can make many different sounds underwater.

Another is that they can make sounds that are heard in the air and underwater at the same time.

That is something no other **mammal** can do.

Some of the sounds hippos make underwater are like clicks. Others sound like croaks or bellows.

More Surprises Ahead

For a hippo to make sounds that are heard both in the air and underwater, the top of its head must be above the water's surface.

The sound that is heard in the air comes from the hippo's **nostrils**.

The sound that is heard underwater comes from the hippo's throat.

Scientists still aren't sure exactly what a hippo's many different sounds mean.

As they go on studying the big-mouthed animals, there are sure to be more surprises to come.

Scientists place microphones in rivers and lakes to record the sounds that hippos make underwater.

Sound Check

Scientists measure how loud or soft sounds are in units called decibels. A male hippo's roar measures about 115 decibels. That's about the same as a train engine. The chart below shows how this level of loudness compares to some other sounds.

Whisper	**Normal Speaking Voice**	**Gas-Powered Lawn Mower**	**Hippo or Train Engine**	**Ambulance Siren**	**Airplane Taking Off**
20 decibels	60 decibels	90 decibels	115 decibels	120 decibels	140 decibels

Glossary

bellowing
(BEL-oh-ing)
making loud,
deep sounds

mammal
(MAM-uhl)
a warm-blooded
animal that has a
backbone, has hair
or fur on its skin, and
drinks its mother's
milk as a baby

nostrils
(NOSS-truhlz)
openings in the
nose that are used
for breathing and
smelling

territory
(TER-uh-*tor*-ee)
an area of land
that belongs to
and is defended
by an animal or a
group of animals

Index

Read More

Pingry, Patricia A. *Baby Hippopotamus (San Diego Zoo Animal Library).* Nashville, TN: CandyCane Press (2004).

Smith, Lucy Sackett. *Hippos: Huge and Hungry (Mighty Mammals).* New York: Rosen (2010).

Storad, Conrad J. *Hippos.* Minneapolis, MN: Lerner (2006).

Learn More Online

To learn more about hippopotamuses, visit
www.bearportpublishing.com/AnimalLoudmouths

About the Author

Natalie Lunis has written many science and nature books for children. She lives in the Hudson River Valley, just north of New York City.